CONTENTS

EXERCISE:A
MASTER HEALER

Exercising Your Mind, Body and Spirit Together, an Excellent Key to a Higher State of Consciousness

Learn why people who engage in Physical, Mental and Spiritual Exercises Lives a Healthier, Younger and Fulfilling Life. Connect to the infinite through simple exercises. Cut years off your Age.

Dr George Akinkuoye

PRIMIX
PUBLISHING
THE WRITE CHOICE

Primix Publishing
11620 Wilshire Blvd
Suite 900, West Wilshire Center, Los Angeles, CA, 90025
www.primixpublishing.com
Phone: 1-800-538-5788

The author of this book does not dispense medical advice nor prescribe the use of any technique as a form of treatment for physical, emotional, or medical problems without the advice of a physician. The intent of the author is only to offer information of a general nature to help you in your quest for emotional and spiritual well-being. In the event you use any of the information in this book for yourself, the author and publisher assume no responsibility for your actions.

Published by Primix Publishing: 04/02/2024

ISBN: 979-8-89194-096-3(sc)
ISBN: 979-8-89194-097-0(e)

Library of Congress Control Number: 2024901272

CHAPTER 1

Introduction

Welcome to the beautiful methods of the ageless wisdom that have been used by many to achieve the mind-body-soul alignment central to excellent human health, inner peace, and a higher state of consciousness.

The idea that exercise is a miracle drug, enhancing health and promoting wellness and longevity, is not new. In 1500 BC, the Olmec civilization in Mexico played a game in which participants used their hips, bottoms, knees, and elbows to move a heavy rubber ball through a ring as a fitness exercise.

In 1400 BC, the pharaohs' tombs depicted the kings' athletic prowess in running, wrestling, and archery competitions through exercises. In 1780, the use of activities in the form of exercise for rehabilitation after surgery and stroke was introduced.

In 1769, William Buchan, a Scottish doctor, was said to have reported that, "Of all the causes which conspire to render the life of man short and miserable, none have greater influence than the want of proper exercise."

Do you ever wonder why so many people start deteriorating after retirement? Too often, retirees pass away after the ability to exercise regularly is abruptly taken away from them. Just as exercising the physical body serves as a preventative measure against sickness and disease of all kinds, activities involving the mind, soul, and spirit prevent diseases of the brain, soul, and spirit.

Most outward manifestations of fear, such as anxiety, chronic headaches, constipation, obesity, PTSD, depression, and many other physical symptoms, have roots in our lack of exercise. Exercises involving cognition and development of the mind not only enhance memory and prevent Alzheimer's, but also shed light on our understanding of the nature of our subconscious being, and the connection between our bodies and body systems.

Daily exercise enhances our dreams, builds our understanding of the soul-mind-body connection, and helps reduce or even eliminates our fear of death and the unknown.

Specific exercises are capable of attuning us to the divine essence that created all, while at the same time strengthening our premonition and monition while alive and dealing with the day-to-day hurdles in our lives.

> *"You have to leave the city of your comfort and go into the wilderness of your intuition. What you'll discover will be wonderful. What you'll discover will be yourself."*
> *– Alan Alda*

The Concepts of Motion

Understanding the concept of motion and its spiritual significance helps shed more light on the reasons movements involving the body, mind, and soul are in line with the influential work and laws of nature. The concept of motion shows why it is crucial to embrace movement and maintain some form of action through engagement in specific types of activities and exercises— both physically and spiritually—rather than be stagnant.

A sedentary life of inactivity, rigidity, and immobility, literally and figuratively, eventually leads to significant problems. A couch-potato lifestyle, sometimes called a parked or neglected-car lifestyle, comes with problems similar to that of a dead battery. It becomes corrosive, warped, and ultimately ineffective, which kills the body and mind and deadens the spirit.

Just as we can be dead in the body, the soul can be stifled, and a life lived with fear, anxiety, depression, anger, and other harmful vices tears us apart on the inside and the outside. Motion and movement in the form of exercise are essential, even during periods of adversity.

All life including the planets are in constant motion

"There are three rules for success. The first: Go on. The second: Go on. And the third: Go on."

– Frank Crane

Just because we get knocked down in life by circumstances that challenge us does not mean we stay knocked down. If we can crawl, then we need to attempt to crawl out of the situation until we can walk away or run from it. In essence, we need to try to move in a positive direction through our actions, our thoughts, and in our minds. Being positive and channeling the energy within our souls in difficult circumstances illuminates the shadows that kept us in despair. Naturally, when light shines, it dispels the shadows.

> *"No problem can be solved from the same consciousness that created it. We must learn to see the world anew."*
>
> **– Albert Einstein**

> *"It's not whether you get knocked down; it's whether you get up."*
>
> **– Vincent Lombardi**

We all have inherent powers we don't yet know how to channel and use. Because we are created in the image of the Supreme Creator, we can achieve goals made by masters and saints of ages past who went through adversities similar to those confronting us today. We must focus, channel our inner resources, and incorporate movement for a more magnificent course.

One of the tenets of quantum physics stipulates that everything in life is in motion and a state of vibration. If life were immobile, it would cease to exist. At both the microscopic and macroscopic levels, movement and vibration exist and are essential to the proper functioning of the systems involved. Changes of such waves from one rate to the other sometimes act as a signal of imbalance in such systems.

Our brains monitor hundreds of oscillations a day in our bodies, ranging from neurotransmitters, the endocrine glands, our body temperature, blood sugar levels, red and white blood cell counts, and many more indicators of health.

The rhythmic motions of our bodies—our heartbeats, sleep cycles, and hormonal cycles—are all movements triggered by other moving parts in our collection of body systems.

The cyclical nature of various events and situations points to the fact that life is immutable. The changing of seasons, ebbs and tides of the ocean, phases of the moon, day and night, and many other examples of lifecycles all point to the perpetual motions of life.

Exercising and engaging the mind, body, and spirit daily aligns with the grand creative forces of nature. This is the key to longevity, health, and wellness of our organization, mind, and soul. Through this book, you will learn firsthand many methods and techniques used by countless enlightened minds throughout the ages to prolong life, build and maintain health and vitality, and stay in tune with the Divine consciousness that pervades the universe and sustains all life.

> *"Nothing in the physical world stays in the same place, or remains what it was; everything moves, everything is going somewhere, is changing inevitably, either develops or goes down, weakens or degenerates... Ascent or descent is the inevitable cosmic condition of any action."*
> *– The Flute of God, Ch. 7*

CHAPTER 2

Exercises for Fitness, Health, and Body Development

The Constitution of Man; Exercise

As humans, we have and carry around so many bodies that are different from the objective, visible, day-to-day body we see and dress. The constitution of man is a full makeup of this physical body of ours, the mind, and a spiritual body (or soul). In other terms, it encompasses your physical or astral body, your causal or etheric mind, and your spiritual body or soul.

Existing also in the physical body are energy centers called chakras or wheels, which keep these bodies active. These energy centers or chakras (spiritual wheels) in the human body correspond to specific organs in the body, which will be discussed a little later in this book. All forms of exercise, whether physical or spiritual, activate these energy centers and keep our bodies alive and healthy.

Our world, whether mortal or immortal, physical or metaphysical, is governed by many spiritual laws. These laws are highly revered by esoteric traditions of the East and West, of which the Ten Commandments and the statutes of sciences are just a little part. According to the law of correspondence, which is one of the vital tenets of nature, "As above, so below." The human physical dimensions are a reflection of things as they occur in the spiritual aspects. Just like our bodies—physical and emotional (astral), causal (memory), mental (mind), and etheric (unconscious)—our souls have a higher spiritual correspondence.

Stretching and relaxing with simple exercise materials.

The physical body is a composition of the chemical elements of the physical plane. It contains a collection of organs and tissues of the body with their respective functions. The human body has more one hundred million cells as the basic unit of life, and these are fundamental building blocks of the body.

The functions and effects of DNA (deoxyribonucleic acid), a highly complex substance formed from the chains of chemical units called nucleotides, are well-known. DNA is the code of life, and it houses the personal, unique genetic information in the nucleus of every cell in the form of chromosomes, which are long strands of DNA molecules.

Studies and revelations of DNA as light by Fritz-Albert Popp and other researchers in recent years allude to the fact that our knowledge about the human body and creation, within which we live and interact daily, is ephemeral.

All systems of the body, from skeletal to muscular, the nervous system, the skin, circulatory, respiratory, endocrine, excretory, reproductive, metabolic, sensory, and immune systems all benefit from exercise when incorporated as a daily routine.

The etheric body is the vehicle of life force, which energizes the physical body and gives it warmth, motion, and sensitivity. It is worth knowing that every form has its etheric counterpart.

The astral body, which is also known as the emotional body, is the source of human feelings. The spiritual correspondence of the astral segment is a plane of a refined state. The astral plane is much larger and more beautiful than the physical plane. It is a plane of psychic phenomenon and commonly mistaken for heaven by those who enter into this plane, in the dream state or through meditation.

The causal body houses memories and has a spiritual counterpart, a causal plane, where memories of past lives and events reside. As understood by many Eastern and esoteric Western religions and organizations, this is where the Akashic record is situated.

The scientific world is still far from understanding these worlds. However, there are currently many scholarly organizations and researchers working in the field of consciousness and dreams, trying to unveil the mysteries behind these planes and human experiences concerning them.

The mental body houses experiences from the mental plane. It is the part that gives a specific character to the personal self in terms of our thought habits and response to circumstances of life. It is associated with all mental functions relating to ideas. The spiritual counterpart of this body is the mental plane, which is the source of the mind and its constructs, such as philosophy, ethics, and moral teachings.

The Intuitional Body (Buddhic or Grand Etheric Body) is the source of human subconscious and first thoughts. The corresponding spiritual plane marks the border between the lower and higher worlds of Divine Spirit.

The soul is known as the higher mind, or Christ within, by many, and it overshadows the human personality. It maintains a direct connection with the man through a thread of energy from the oversoul. The human physical form is mortal, but the soul immortal. It is capable of linking Spirit (Divine) and matter (body) in what is called (at-one-ment) or atonement through spiritual exercises. It's important to understand that the immortal soul should dominate and direct the mortal body for a proper soul-mind-body alignment through activities.

Exercise material for body and leg stimulation.

Exercises for Physical Fitness

It is no coincidence that dogs and cats and many other animals stretch when they wake up. Physical activity plays a significant role in our health and wellness and, through daily activities, affects many areas of our lives, such as the somatic, cognitive, emotive, appetite, physiological, and psychological states of the body.

Many somatic complaints are associated with a sedentary lifestyle and a lack of exercise. When individual movement is impeded, death is imminent. It is no surprise that necrosis and ulcers develop from immobility. Hospitals and nursing facilities globally advocate frequent repositioning for this reason.

Doing everything possible to engage in some form of movement is vital to life sustenance. The American Heart Association recommends healthy adults engage in 30 minutes of moderate exercise at least five days per week and 25 minutes of vigorous activity three times a week.

Many health establishments all over the world spend so much money on treating diseases rather than encouraging preventative measures such as exercise. Through regular activities, many illnesses treated, along with their associated health care costs, would have been eliminated, says Dr. Jordan Metzl, a New York sports medicine physician.

According to Dr. Sylvia R Karasu, in her article titled A Body in Motion: Exercise and Cognition." Retrieved from PsychologyToday.com on October 30, 2019. She illustrated how exercises improve cognition. Regular activities could slow the progression of Alzheimer's diseases. Studies in humans and animals strongly support the neuroprotective effect of the use on Aerobic activities that depend on oxygen use, like swimming and cycling, or anaerobic exercises, such as jumping or weight lifting, that involve a burst of energy performed with maximum effort, have a neuroprotective effect on cognition.

Other researchers have called exercise a vascular medicine (Green and Smith, Cold Spring Harbour Perspectives in Medicine, 2018).

A 95 year old grandmother
exercising for good health.

Research shows that the volume of the hippocampus in the human brain, which is responsible for memory, is increased by exercise. Exercise also increases synaptic plasticity and blood flow to the brain, decreasing age-related brain atrophy in many areas.

Exercise increases the synthesis and release of neurotrophins and growth factors. Hence, physical exercise offers protection against cognitive decline by inducing both neurochemicals and structural changes within the brain (<u>A Body in Motion: Exercise and Cognition | Psychology Today</u>, retrieved October 30, 2019).

Exercising the physical body helps with weight loss, blood sugar and blood pressure regulation, increased stamina and balance, increasing the body's high-density lipoprotein (HDL) cholesterol, and decreasing the low-density lipoprotein (LDL), which is the bad cholesterol.

Other effects of exercise are strengthening the immune system, lessening the frequency of asthma attacks, reducing chronic pain, improving mood, enhancing the heart, and supporting longevity.

Examples of simple aerobic exercises are:

- Walking
- Jogging
- Aerobic dancing
- Basketball
- Skiing

Examples of anaerobic exercises:

- Weightlifting
- Sprinting
- High-intensity interval training
- Jump squats
- Box jumps

CHAPTER 3

Exercises for Unlocking the Secrets of Your Dreams

The Effects of Exercise on Sleep Quality and Dreams

Exercise significantly influences sleep quality and dreams. Historically, perhaps no daytime behavior has been more closely associated with better sleep than exercise (Youngstedt, 2005). Engaging in specific dream exercises and techniques individually— apart from general physical body exercise—falls in line with the concept of motion and movements.

Exercises involving our mental faculties and the mind have the capability of helping in the understanding of dreams, and increasing the frequency and capability of recalls. It is a method used throughout the ages by many advanced souls. Learning the types of exercises to do and engaging in daily practice have multiple beneficial effects. Dreams are capable of bringing precognition and direct cognition of events before they occur. Some consider dreams to be windows to the soul and to eternity.

Understanding different methods of working with

dreams offers the potential to relieve so many individuals of nightmares and bad dreams, while at the same time presenting opportunities to work with such thoughts and learn how to use them to resolve conflicts and dissolve karmic debts.

Dreams are an essential part of the sleeping process. Yet unfortunately, many are unable to remember if they dreamed, and so are not able to take advantage of this opportunity of unlocking the secrets of their dreams. One of the benefits of dreaming and understanding it is the ability to use the messages in problem-solving. Our dreams, whether disguised in symbols or through direct communication without symbolic representations, can relay vital information about our health and areas where attention is needed.

Mainly, recurring dreams, according to Vasili Kasatkin, a Russian researcher, are early warning signs of events and occurrences. Dreams are used successfully by many for discovering lost items; for purification purposes, tapping into the subconscious to elicit a creative idea; enhancing love lives; and foretelling future events, to list but a few.

A notable example of a predictive dream is that of Abraham Lincoln's. He dreamed of a body, lying in state in the White House, surrounded by people. When he asked who died, a soldier replied, "It was the President... killed by the assassin."

So many people dreamed about September 11th, earthquakes in Haiti, and volcanic eruptions in Hawaii, and woke up to the realities of these events a few days later.

Dreams preceded many creative and scientific discoveries:

- Albert Einstein came to the scientific

development of the principle of relativity after a vivid dream.

- A self-described mathematical genius, Snivasa Ramanujan said his insights on the analytical theory of numbers were from dreams.
- Mary Shelley, writer of the first sci-fi novel in 1816, was inspired by a vivid nightmare.
- In 1965, Paul McCartney said the entire melody for his hit acoustic song, "Yesterday," was written in a dream.
- The father of quantum mechanics, Neils Bohr, often spoke of the dream that led to his discovery of the atom structure.

"Dreams are illustrations from the book your soul is writing about you."

– Marsha Norman

Dream Exercises and Their Benefits

Dream Exercises: Technique 1

- **Step 1**

   Get a notepad and pen to begin journaling your dreams.

- **Step 2**

   If you think you do not dream, get an alarm clock, and set it at some specific time, like 1 or 2 a.m. Wake up when your alarm rings and quietly contemplate the contents of your dream before being woken up by the alarm. Do this consistently every night until you can remember it. Write this down immediately.

- **Step 3**

   Write down the date and time of the dream and give it a title.

- **Step 4**

   Write in the present tense to keep the story of the dream active.

- **Step 5**

   When you awake, do not rush to get up, but lie down or sit for a few minutes to connect with your dream.

- **Step 6**

   Quickly write down any questions that come to mind.

- **Step 7**

   Keep note of any odors, colors, or sounds while recording your dreams as these may be an essential part of the communication. As an example, a lady called

Jane had recurrent dreams of smoke in her sleep for three weeks in a row, only to find her apartment burned down four weeks later while she was at work.

Specific colors may be meaningful interpretations of your dreams. Typical colors associated with particular events are:

Gray: Suggesting cloudiness or situations that are unclear; also interpreted as fright, depression, or poor health

Yellow: Associated with well-being and intellect

Red: Interpreted as anger, power, aggression, and a stop signal

White: Holiness, purity, peace

Purple: Spirituality, healing tendencies

Blue: Eternity, tranquility

Black: Hidden, the unknown, death

Orange: Energy, friendliness

Green: Hope, growth, green light to go ahead

- **Step 8**
Avoid caffeine, alcohol, and drugs, which are known as REM sleep suppressants.

- **Step 9**
Tell yourself repeatedly during the day that you will remember your dreams.

- **Step 10**
Do not share your dreams, as each person's dreams are unique, except with your dream partner, in a dream group, or with a dream teacher.

Dream Exercises: Technique 2

Connecting the Physical Body to the Vibrations of the Dream State

- **Step 1**
If you belong to a spiritual group that uses prayer, meditation, or chants such as "Ohm," "Hu," "Alleluia," etc., using this daily before going to bed will enhance dream quality.

- **Step 2**
Find a comfortable chair with a straight back to sit on or lie down.

- **Step 3**
Close your eyes, and begin focusing on the blind spot between your eyebrows.

- **Step 4**
Chant your familiar word of choice or prayer for 5 minutes, then stay silent, still focusing on this spot. If you are not familiar with any of this, simply focus on the place for approximately 5 to 10 minute.

- **Step 5**
Take a deep breath through the nose and expel slowly through the nose three times. Then visualize a blue light and stream of energy radiating straight out from your blind spot or third eye area into infinite space.

- **Step 6**

Say a concluding affirmation, prayer, or blessing of your choice and add that the blessings of the Divine Spirit guide and protect you through the dream process while you sleep. Take a slow, deep breath and let it out through your nose, relaxing and going to sleep, surrendering to the Divine Providence for protection.

Dream Exercises: Technique 3

For Lucid Dream Travel

- **Step 1**

Lie on your back in a dimly lighted or a dark room, not too bright to cause distractions.

- **Step 2**

Close your eyes and relax completely, taking slow, natural breaths; become aware of the rhythm of your breathing.

- **Step 3**

Place your attention on a spot on the upper part of your eyelid. Focus on a single spot, concentrating on the blackness above each eyelid, for 5 to 10 minutes.

- **Step 4**

Next, shift your focus upward, concentrating on a point approximately 12 inches (30 cm) above your forehead, gradually extending the distance from your forehead up to the ceiling and beyond.

- **Step 5**

Using your faculties of imagination and visualization, see the beauty of any kind that comes to mind. Imagine how beautiful it would be floating or flying around in space to a place of interest like a celestial garden or a beach that transcends time and space.

- **Step 6**

  Daily practices of this technique will make it easier with time and strengthen the practitioner's ability to engage in out-of-body dream travel every night. This daily practice will also enhance your ability to recall your dreams.

- **Step 7**

  Stepping back into your body is as easy as thinking of your body and your room, and you will find yourself again in the physical awareness of where you are.

Dream Exercises: Technique 4

Influencing Dream Outcomes

Positive dream outcomes are capable of being created, using positive mental health techniques and mind power to create positive dreaming outcomes.

A negative dream experience can be turned into a positive one simply by entering into a meditative mood and putting yourself back into the adverse dream event as distinctly as you can. Remember it and recreate it with your mind, making it end the way you want.

As an example, if you have a nightmare of being chased or a nightmare of failure in an exam, do the following:

- **Step 1**

  Find a quiet place to relax.

- **Step 2**
  Take three slow, deep breaths through your nose and expel through your nose. Do this gently and slowly.

- **Step 3**
  Say a protective prayer or chant for 5 minutes.

- **Step 4**
  Recreate the dream, using as much as you can remember of the details.

- **Step 5**
  Reverse the dream piece by piece, making each segment of the dream end as you want it to. Your visualization of how you want it to conclude must be your focus, with faith, as it is accomplished. If you need to chase the person who was chasing you, do so and imagine them running. If you need to sit for an exam, do so by recreating it in your mind, then see everyone congratulating you for passing the exam.

- **Step 6**
  Take another three deep breaths in through your nose and gently expel through your nose.

- **Step 7**
  Say your final prayer of appreciation or final chant to seal the event.

- **Step 8**
  Arise and dismiss the event from your mind, going about your daily activities. Do not give it any thought again, nor be afraid, nor doubt yourself.

CHAPTER 4

The Power of Mindfulness Exercises And Their Effects on the Imagination and Spoken Words

The Mind and Its Attributes

M indfulness living is an essential method that not only helps in mind control, but is a technique capable of bringing abundant joy, focus, and calm into our everyday life, rather than being buffeted around, a victim of our own minds and circumstances. The mind plays an essential role in the full realization of the benefits and rewards of other exercises. We humans can be masters of our mind, utilizing them for higher achievements, rather than servants blown around by the destructive forces caused by distorted thoughts.

"Happiness is when what you think, what you say, and what you do are in harmony."
– Mahatma Gandhi

Due to the emergence and full dependency on

electronic gadgets like cell phones, it is unfortunate to see that so many people are no longer able to memorize or remember phone numbers of their close acquaintances. The area of the brain that deals with the learning of facts and figures—the hippocampus, which is part of the limbic system—becomes dormant.

What we don't use, we lose. Hence, doing simple, daily exercises, like memorizing numbers and words, doing a puzzle, or other mental stimuli, goes a long way in reactivating the memory cells in the brain. Many religions use things like the rosary and other prayer aids to help anchor the mind on the subject at hand. Such practices are exercises, beyond the spiritual benefits to the practitioners. They help activate and keep your memory cells active.

Another dimension of the mind is that relating to the effects of our thought life. Studies show that the human brain is capable of distorted thought forms, that our thoughts are potent, and have both productive and destructive capabilities.

Being mindful of our thoughts at all times is highly recommended, as we become that which we think. Positive thoughts attract positive attributes, while negative thoughts bind us to negative ones.

> *The road is smooth. Why do you throw rocks before you?*
> **– Ancient expression**

What do you think about when you physically exercise? Are your thoughts positive and creative, or are they harmful and destructive? Exercising mindfulness as a way of living in your daily life not only makes your physical activity more rewarding, but also adds the beauty and full benefits of mindfulness, such as living with abundant joy and an inner peace.

Are you hindered by a tsunami of rising thoughts, not able to stop and enjoy the moment? With the quality and content of your thinking, you can undo the benefits of your exercises or uplift them. Focusing on beauty, either of nature or that of music and positive attributes, allows you to reap the full benefits of your exercises. Listen to empowering music, think of the people you love, and remember happy experiences or that of watching a favorite motivating show while you exercise can help prevent the mind from reverting to negative self-analysis and racing thoughts of troubling situations. Thoughts of love, gratitude, compassion, and compliments of others work to increase physical awareness of your body and bring inner strength.

> *"The way you think, the way you behave, the way you eat can influence your life by 30 to 50 years."*
> **– Deepak Chopra**

Just as there are exercises for building body muscle and physical strength or for weight loss, similarly, there are exercises for building up your mind. These types of activities develop the mind and allow it to be a proper conduit for the mind-body-soul alignment.

Basic simple exercises, such as working with word puzzles, playing chess, and other similar games, help improve mental cognition and prevent early onset of dementia, including Alzheimer's. These types of activities keep your brain cells active and in shape, just as physical exercises will for the physical body.

Apart from these basic cognitive exercises, numerous

others activate the link between our bodies, allowing them to communicate more freely with each other.

Yoga as an Exercise

There are numerous exercises for the development of the mind in every culture and religion. One of the most popular ones, yoga, originated from Northern India from the Indus-Savarati civilization more than 5,000 years ago. In contrast, modern-day yoga, which is widely practiced by so many, started in the early 1800s.

When people think of yoga, they automatically think of physical exercise. Although physical activity is an intrinsic part of yoga, the meaning and effects extend far beyond physical exercise alone.

Yoga is also a mental and spiritual practice that puts the mind in shape just as it does with the body. The word "yoga" means yoke, that is, uniting or syncing of body and mind through posture, breathing, and meditation.

The pose, which is also known as Asana, is carefully combined with the breathing method called Pranayama. You do not need to master all the various positions to benefit from yoga.

In a national survey reported by the Harvard Medical School,

nearly 4% of adults in the United States engaged in the practice of yoga in 2016, while approximately one in three have tried it at least once in their lifetime. From 10 million Americans practicing yoga in 2016 to an estimated 36 million participating in 2022, its popularity cannot be overstated.

There are many different types of yoga. Central to some of these yoga methods are the eight limbs of yoga. In the second century, Patanjali, an advocate of

Raja Yoga, detailed in his classic book the eight limbs of the salient part of yoga as: Yama (Abstinence), Niyama (Observance), Asana (Posture), Pranayama (Breath Control), Pratyahara (Withdrawal), Dharana (Concentration), Dhyana (Meditation), and Samadhi (Bliss or Enlightenment).

Exercises for the Development of Your Mind

Memory Test Exercises for Inner Awareness Recognition

- **Step 1**
  As you move about during the day, pay close attention to the details of everything you see—the forms, the colors, any smells or odors—and sounds heard, if any. When you walk into a room, study what is hanging on the wall, the colors, the objects around the room, the lighting, and furnishings, etc.

- **Step 2**
  Do a memory recall daily sometime in the evening to see how many of the details you can remember.

- **Step 3**
  Do this in a nonjudgmental way, irrespective of what you have seen earlier. Do not berate yourself or get upset if you cannot recall as many details as you think you should.

  These exercises help strengthen the memory cells involved, which, in turn, allow the practitioner to develop an ability to recall their dreams and occurrences while out of the body at night when sleeping.

Body Awareness Scan

The body scan awareness method is a technique used by mystics and saints in ages past for energizing the cells of the body, while at the same time invoking their sensitivity and increasing the awareness of all the body parts involved, based on the principle that thought is energy. It has been used or programmed to heal diseased areas or communicate with a particular body part. Each body part has its duty, and your thoughts and mind awaken the dormant body parts into action.

- **Step 1**
  Begin by sitting comfortably on a chair with your legs down below, resting gently on the floor, and keeping them apart. Gently place the palm of your hands on your lap.

- **Step 2**
  Close your eyes, if you like, to prevent distractions

and take a slow deep breath in through the nose, and gently breathe out through the nose. Repeat this three times slowly.

- **Step 3**
Concentrate on your lower body parts, starting with your left or right leg, while taking a slow deep breath simultaneously as you are focus on that body part.

- **Step 4**
Release your breath, and take in another deep breath through the nose. Slowly work your concentration up and focus on all other body parts—the knees, the thighs, the stomach, liver, spleen, the colons, all the other internal organs of the body, and the arms— while exhaling and inhaling slowly with each concentration.

- **Step 5**
Continue concentration and breaths for all body parts, working your way to the head and center of the skull or crown of the head. Be aware of each body part as you inhale and exhale. Complete the exercise, then sit in silence for 5 to 10 minutes before you dismiss.

Another variation of the above exercise is called Body Circuit Energy storage:

- **Step 1**
In this exercise, you have to stand with your arms stretched out beside you.

- **Step 2**
Take a deep breath and visualize the energy moving from the ground you are standing on, passing into your feet, your legs, and running through your back and neck in a straight line up to the top of your head in the center.

- **Step 3**
As you exhale, see the energy descending through your face and neck, down through your chest, and flowing into the navel area as you complete the breathing.

Anger Inoculation (Balloon Technique)

This is an anger management protocol that will help you stabilize your mind and rid yourself of toxic thought patterns. When something provokes anger in someone, the sympathetic nervous system of the person provoked is heightened to a higher arousal level, such as in a fight-or-flight response. The anger inoculation method will assist in lowering this arousal level, through the steps below. This method gives you effective coping skills capable of helping you prevent reoccurrence when practiced at the first signs of provoking thoughts or images. It is similar to the anger inoculation protocol developed by Defenbacher and McKay, 2000.

This method involves the use of relaxation skills, coping thoughts, inoculation, and the formulation of a real-life coping plan through the method.

- **Step 1**
Find a comfortable place to sit with your spine supported. Breath flows more freely when the body is aligned. Rest your hands comfortably on your lap.

- **Step 2**
Inhale through your nose and feel your belly expand. Do not move the chest. Hold as long as you comfortably can, then exhale, breathing out the air completely.

- **Step 3**

  Develop anger coping thoughts, such as recognizing that no human being is perfect, and that you yourself are not perfect. Remind yourself of the good side of others you may not know yet. Counsel yourself that, even though the situation is irritating, it will be history tomorrow. Recognize that you cannot change others; you can only change and control yourself.

- **Step 4**

  Take in a slow, deep breath through your nose while thinking of the offending situation that triggered the anger. Visualize a big red balloon and blow it up, emptying all your anger into the balloon. Continue to exhale until you see the balloon burst into pieces in your imagination through visualization. While visualizing the anger energy, say the following, 'As this inflated balloon has burst, so also has the negative energy in my mind.'

- **Step 5**

  Develop an action plan on how to manage day-to-day provocations that could lead to anger, and a timetable of daily, quarterly, or monthly practice, if needed.

Game of Chess Exercise for Anxiety and Stress Reduction (Used for Solving Difficult Situations)

This exercise can be done at any time, whether you are at work or at home, during contemplation, or at night when you can't sleep.

- **Step 1**

  Focus your attention on the troubling situation.

- **Step 2**
Take a deep breath in through your nose, hold it in as long as you can, then release it gently by exhaling through the nose.

- **Step 3**
Focus your attention on the crown chakra on top of the head for 5 to 10 minutes. Inwardly chant your preferred spiritual word like Hu, Alleluia, Jesus, Hosanna, and visualize yourself rising into this region above time and space in your soul body.

- **Step 4**
Look down on the problem and, seeing it as a chess game, carefully rearrange it into the position you want it to be in. See the end result as being accomplished without worrying about the outcome.

- **Step 5**
Inhale gently, holding it in as long as tolerated, and gently exhale.

- **Step 6**
Once the exercise is completed, dismiss the entire process from your mind, believing that the outcome will be beneficial. More positive results are achieved through this method as the consciousness becomes elevated through daily meditation and spiritual exercises. Meditation and spiritual exercises practiced regularly for as little as 5 minutes every day improves the outcome beyond your imagination.

Exercises for Regaining Emotional Balance

This exercise will help you regain emotional balance, especially if you have to interact or work with people whom you have a negative attitude about.

- **Step 1**
  When meeting or working around people whom you have negative feelings about, for one reason or another, mentally and silently say to yourself, "In the name of God, I bless this meeting or I bless this person." Other words such as Sugmad, Allah, Christ, and so on can be substituted, depending on your faith.)

- **Step 2**
  Be polite when they are around you, but silently chant a spiritual word of power, such as Hu, Ohm, Alleluia, Maranatha, and so on. Listen to them, but mentally chant your word as you listen without saying much.

- **Step 3**
  If you need to look at them at all, and you are not comfortable doing this, simply focus on the bridge of their nose while you chant your word silently.

- **Step 4**
  Visualize your spiritual guide or a holy person of choice as being next to you, depending on your faith. As a Christian, you can visualize Christ.
  When you bless a situation, you are keeping yourself emotionally balanced. You are shielded from a negative karmic emotional entanglement.

Stress Relief Relaxation Exercise

Are you using a time-tested stress management technique available to help in your quick relaxation process?

Place one hand on your chest, place the other hand on your stomach. Breathe normally for approximately thirty to forty seconds. If the hand placed on your chest is moving, then you are like many others probably not taking advantage of this relaxation techniques that has helped many.

Breathing condition most of the body processes. It affects the whole body. When anyone is angry, it is a usual occurrence that the breathing becomes irregular, as stress and fear triggers quick and shallow breathing. On the contrary, an ideal relaxed state is usually characterized by slow, deep and regular breathing. Taking a few seconds to breathe slowly, deeply, and regularly when faced with a stressful situation will not only help produce a state of relaxation, but it will also help to build a respiratory reserve common to most breathing exercises, and increase the capacity of the blood to carry oxygen throughout the circulatory system. This type of corrected breathing pattern will help short-circuit the stress response and promote comfort and relaxation. It allows the diaphragm to respond in the appropriate way, by expanding downward when we inhale, allowing the stomach to gently expand outward.

Exercise for Reducing Stress

When faced with a stressful situation anywhere anytime, do the following:

- **Step 1**
Stand or sit as erect as possible, and try to take your mind off of stressful situations or activities as much as you can.

- **Step 2**
Take a slow, deep breath while counting to three.

- **Step 3**
Hold your breath gently for a count of three.

- **Step 4**
Exhale slowly for a count of three.

- **Step 5**
Pause for a count of three.

- **Step 6**
Repeat the sequence again three times.

- **Step 7**
Return to your activities.

Making Relaxation Response Techniques a Way of Life

Relaxation response requires certain vital conditions be in place to be effective.

Having a quiet time and place are as essential to the success of the system as the techniques themselves. It is vital to choose a time and place where you will not be disturbed. Using the same place at the same time of day is helpful. Your special place can be a physical place or an imaginary place and your space should be considered as such.

For a daily habit of practice, avoid practicing the techniques immediately before retiring, as you will probably fall asleep, or after a meal, as the body will be occupied with the digestive process, which prevents adequate concentration and relaxation.

Be in a comfortable position during the exercise. Use your favorite chair or sofa, but with your back straight as much as you can, with your head and neck supported, if possible.

A word or phrase of choice to act as an anchor for the mind is helpful, as this helps prevent distractions. Phrases commonly used are: I am calm, I am a strand of light, I am relaxing, I am a renewed person, I am a healing energy, I am loved, Divine love, shelter me, my mind is quiet.

A positive and passive attitude is essential in the learning process as you follow the instructions.

Mental Shift Relaxation Technique

- **Step 1**
Select a comfortable sitting or reclining position, or a seated position you prefer.

- **Step 2**
Close your eyes, and think about a place near or remote, a place of interest you may have been before, or any other beautiful place of choice you can vividly imagine. (This place should be a quiet, peaceful environment.)

- **Step 3**
Imagine that you are now in this ideal, rejuvenating location; endeavor to be present there at this moment

in time. Imagine all the colors, the smells, and sounds of this environment.

- **Step 4**

  Feel the peace, the calmness of this place, and immerse yourself in it fully, imagining your body, mind, and spirit being transformed and rejuvenated by this place.

- **Step 5**

  After about 10 minutes, slowly open your eyes, stretch, and try to gradually bring back your experiences to your current physical, wakeful location.

Life never goes in a straight line, and never will. There will always be ups and downs, ebbs and tides, the bear market and the bull markets, the births and the deaths, the days and nights of life, as clearly made visible to us in nature by the Divine. We must learn from nature and work with nature as much as we can to keep ourselves within the healing, positive alignments of nature. Resistance to the laws of nature that surround us only brings pain and suffering. However, we can learn to work within the laws of nature, understand the laws, and be cooperative and creative within the laws without letting down our guard when faced with misfortunes and trying moments, which are the valleys of life.

Remember that you can build an imaginary, ideal castle and a place of sanctity to visit as often as needed or during moments of crises as you wish.

> **"Life is like a roller coaster. You can either scream every time there is a bump or you can throw your hands up and enjoy the ride."**
> **– Unknown**

CHAPTER 5

The Soul and The Spirit Interaction in Man

The Nature of the Soul and the Spirit in Man

A review of the spiritual texts and holy books of most religion shows the soul to be eternal, with no beginning and no end. The majority of the Holy Scriptures the world over have the common belief that the soul is the spiritual entity in man, and some theologians and denominations in both East and West commonly believe that human makeup consists of body, soul, and spirit.

The purpose of this book is not for debating theological doctrines, but to point to the salient fact that, just as the human body exercises to get in shape and ward off illnesses, spiritual practices involving the soul and spirit help ward off extraneous energy and negative influences that are not in alignment with the purposes for which the soul, in incarnation, were created.

This book does not delve into the type of spiritual path or religion you choose to follow, as that is between you and your Creator. Its sole purpose is that your soul become aware of its true divinity through exercises and the practice of other virtues as they may relate to the uplifting of the carnal man from the physical into the spiritual realms.

Just as the nature of the soil determines the vitality and the vibrant quality of a growing plant, and what is beneath the ground and not discernible by the naked eye is a powerful determinant of the survival of the plant, the same principle applies to human life on earth. There are many subjective influences in life, both negative and positive that, although not seen, have a powerful impact on human beings. These forces, more often than not, determine our state and survival in life.

The physical exercises of the body and its parts alone will not cause the soul-body-mind alignment to be achieved; all the other components of the human makeup, such as the spirit and the soul, must be focused on the sense of at-one-ment.

> *"Our body and our minds can take us only so far. Our Spirit can lead us all the way home."*
> **– Susan Jeffers**

Central to discussions about the body and the soul are the energy centers called chakras. They help readers understand some of the spiritual exercises presented below, as they involve the energy centers in the human body.

"Chakra" means wheel in Sanskrit. Chakras are circular centers of subtle energy in the human body that correspond to the nerve plexuses and organs in the physical nervous system. There are seven major chakras, and each has its respective function in the human body. The names are given below in Sanskrit:

1. **Muladhara**: This is the seat of primal life energy. It resides at the base of the spine and sacral

plexus, and is associated with the organs of excretion. It is the earth

2. **Swadhisthana**: This is the center and the seat of creativity. It is located in the genitals and prostatic plexus and is associated with the gonads. It is the water element.

3. **Manipura**: This is the seat of the will, ego, feelings, and subconscious emotions. It resides at the navel and solar plexus, and is associated with the pancreas and abdominal organs. It is the fire element.

4. **Anahata**: This is the heart center. It is the seat of love and is located at the heart and cardiac plexus, and is associated with the thymus and lungs. It is the air element.

5. **Vishudha**: This is the seat of creative expression and communication. It is located in the throat and laryngeal plexus, and is associated with the thyroid. It is the ether element.

6. **Ajna**: This is located between the eyebrows, in the cavernous plexus, and is associated with the pituitary gland. It is commonly referred to as the "third eye," and is associated with the primordial power of the soul.

7. **Sahasrara or the thousand-petal lotus**: This is called the crown chakra. It is the center of illumination and divine love and oneness with all. This is in the brain and is associated with the pineal gland. The crown chakra is commonly called the region of the liberated souls dwelling in eternal bliss. It possesses all powers.

There are physical, measurable electromagnetic and magnetic fields generated by all living tissue, cells, organs, and there are also bio-fields, which are subtle

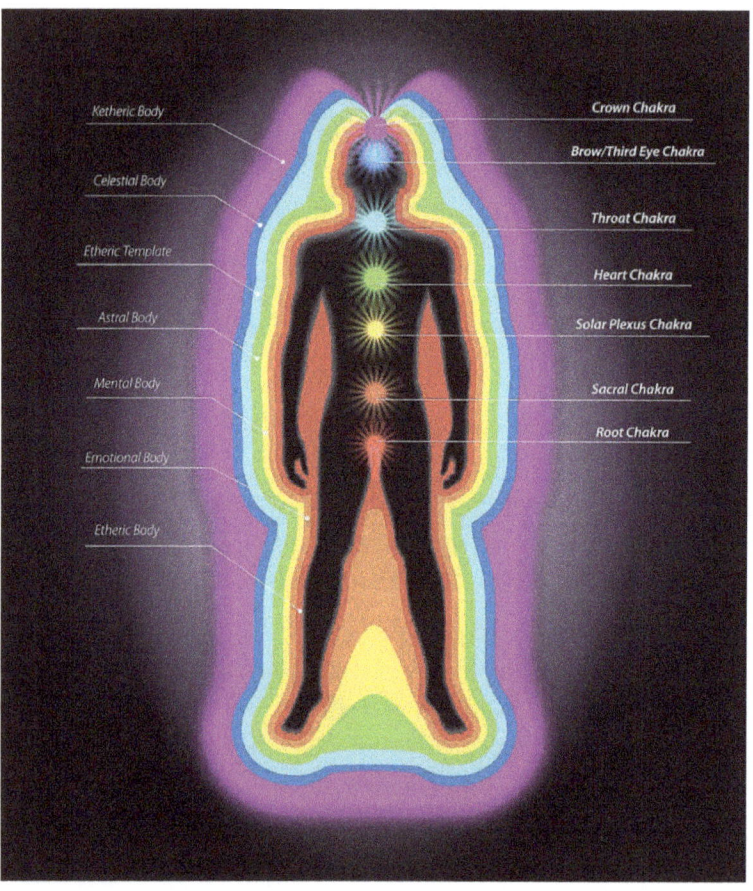

energy related to the chakras described above. Each field of energy is made active and expanded through both physical and spiritual exercises with their resultant vibrant health and clarity of mind and receptivity.

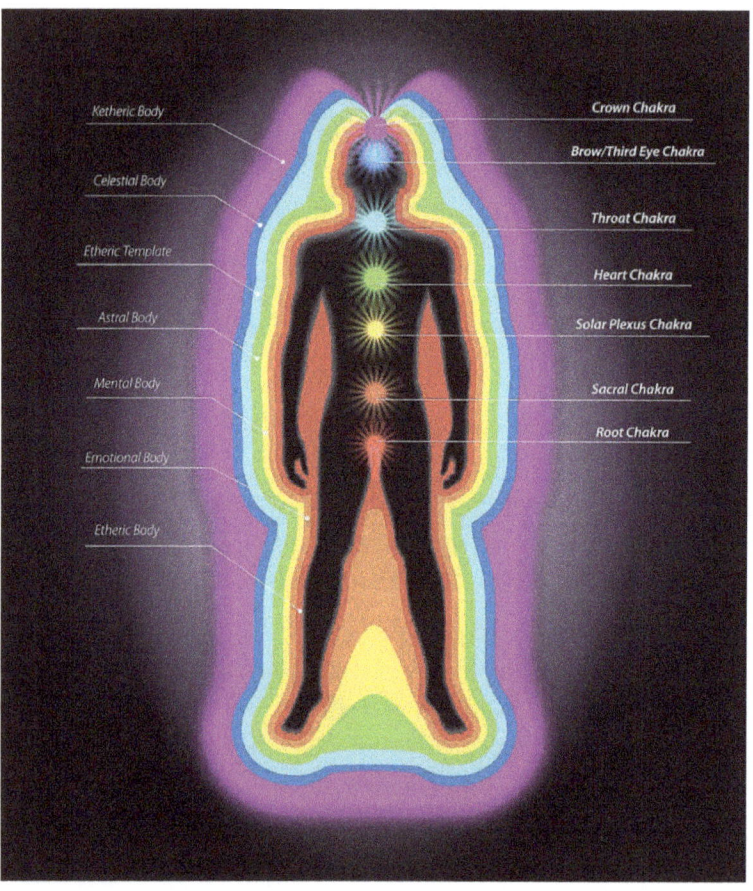

Ketheric Body

Celestial Body

Etheric Template

Astral Body

Mental Body

Emotional Body

Etheric Body

Crown Chakra

Brow/Third Eye Chakra

Throat Chakra

Heart Chakra

Solar Plexus Chakra

Sacral Chakra

Root Chakra

Some basic yoga spiritual exercises are known to have the capability of developing the spirit while connecting to the higher self and direct experiences of the soul.

Many followers of other faiths and religions also have their ways of achieving some degree of alignment, either through prayer, meditation, or contemplation. Catholics speak of the spiritual exercises of Ignatius Loyola, a Catholic saint.

There are other ancient practices of the Eastern Orthodox Catholic Church such as Hesychasm, a mystical, traditional contemplative, and meditative prayer with numerous adaptations for modern use.

The Lectio Divina, a Latin word for Divine Reading, is a traditional monastic exercise of Scriptoral reading, meditation, and prayer designed to promote communion with God. This method advocates studying Scripture as the living word, rather than as a text. It has four steps comprised of reading, meditation, prayer, and contemplation. The root of this method goes back to the third century. Saint Ambrose, Augustine of Hippo, and Saint Benedict of Nursia are among many others who used this method. This technique was recommended to the general public in the 20th century by the Second Vatican Council.

Whichever path we choose, it is necessary to be aware that each has its limitations. The central fact of this course is that, rather than only focusing on exercises that promote a carnal cause, it is enlightenment working toward the awareness of soul contact, which allows us the attributes of the soul-body-spirit alignment.

We know the physical body withers over time as it is temporal, while our spiritual bodies endure beyond the physical world.

One of the exercises that is both fascinating and useful is called Karma Buster (unification exercise). This technique is presented below. It helps the practitioner achieve oneness with their higher self, the soul, while simultaneously assisting the practitioner in dissolving negative karmic patterns as it involves blessing others and blessing the earth to amend things and dissolve negative karmic energy patterns. We all have people we have offended, people who hurt us, nationalities and cities and situations we dislike, etc.

Such energy patterns bind us to others, to a particular area or specific situation. Dissolving this karmic encounter through this recommended method will not only help dissolve the negative bond, but also facilitate a quicker connection with our divine soul. It is a meditation on lovingkindness. It is used for blessing an individual, a place, a company, a country, or a region where you have karmic ties or just as a token of love.

When done regularly, this exercise is capable of affording the practitioner better physical, emotional, mental, and positive spiritual health. As you bless, so you are also blessed. It is better to be a blessing than a curse. This exercise has been used as part of the ageless wisdom and techniques employed by masters and saints to help activate both the heart and the crown chakra in a faster format than any other method.

These two chakras are seldom activated in many, as formal education places no emphasis on them. There are different versions of this technique with special chants like ohm or hu used with breathing exercises. Christians can use Christ, Jesus, maranatha, alleluia, kyrie, etc. Still, the simplified version presented here has been used daily by many with successful results.

Exercises for the Development of Your Soul and Spirit Unification Exercise Technique and Karma Buster

- **Step 1**

Do a brief physical exercise of your choice like stretching, briefly jogging, stretching your arms and legs to cleanse the etheric body (optional).

- **Step 2**

  Sit on a comfortable chair with your back erect, hands face-down or upward, resting on your lap. Say a brief protective invocation or prayer of your choice depending on your faith and spiritual inclination.

- **Step 3**

  Visualize a brilliant white or golden light of energy radiating from your heart center, shining, pulsating, and radiating through the cells in your heart. The heart is a unique organ of love. The elements that divide humans, such as a bridge or a wall, resides in the heart center. The seed of karma emanates from here. Visualize this pulsating light radiating from the center to the other parts of the entire body. Slowly inhale, hold it as long as you comfortably can, then slowly exhale.

- **Step 4**

  Visualize a brilliant white or golden light, radiating and connecting to the head center at the top of your head (the crown chakra region). Visualize the white or golden light from the divine plane higher above coming straight down through your head center into your body. Take a deep breath, hold it as long as you comfortably can, then release it.

- **Step 5**

  After energizing both the heart and the head centers for as long as tolerable, visualize a person, a city, or the Earth as a globe and the area you wish to bless.

  Raise the palm and visualize the powerful golden energy of light radiating to the imagined person and environment. Repeat softly "May the divine power that sustains all life purify and bless (substitute the name of the region or the person) and dissolve any negative karmic patterns that may be holding back divine manifestation according to the Divine will.

Divine Father, I pardon everyone who has offended me and also ask for forgiveness of my errors of omission and commission. Divine Father, make me an instrument of your peace and let me continue to show love and bring light and hope to others and the world." Take another slow, deep breath, hold it, then slowly release.

- **Step 6**
Repeat a closing prayer or recitation of your choice.

> *"Direct your eye inward, and you'll find A thousand regions in your mind Yet undiscovered. Travel them, and be Expert in home-cosmography."*
> **– Henry David Thoreau**

Exercise of Surrender and Complete Healing (Experiencing the Infinite)

- **Step 1**
Sit down in a comfortable chair with your back supported. Recite the following: "Divine Light, Divine Love, light my life and heal me in and out. I hereby invoke Thy Divine Presence for full protection and guidance as I heal and recreate myself anew for Thy purposes. I dispel all negative energy patterns around me. I forgive anyone who has ever offended me and ask for forgiveness of my errors of omission and commission to anyone.

- **Step 2**
Take a deep breath through the nose, hold it as long as you comfortably can, then exhale (Do this three times).

- **Step 3**
  Visualize a mountain of light in your inner eye. See it and make it real through your visualization.

- **Step 4**
  Visualize yourself walking toward this mountain. Climb the mountain until you reach the top.

- **Step 5**
  While on the mountain top, visualize your guide, or your creator in a dazzling brilliant color in whichever image comes to mind. Say the following: I release all my earthly worries and early equipment, my body into the divine spirit for recreation anew. Make me a new person and heal all my maladies and imperfections.
  See your body becoming lighter and see it as a woven thread of cells. Where you are is sacred ground, a purified region beyond time and space; it is a spiritual dimension.

- **Step 6**
  Begin to dismantle the threads that make up your body one by one, until you merge with the Infinite Spirit. See yourself as one with the Divine Spirit who creates all. Take a deep breath through the nose, hold it as long as you comfortably can, then exhale.

- **Step 7**
  Visualize your Guide helping you mold a new form, a new body from the divine elements of the spiritual dimension, as a living soul in His image. Visualize the divine attribute you want to develop. Maintain an attitude of completion that these qualities are already in place, and end the session with a little prayer or chant of your choice. Thank your Guide or Creator, whichever you use, for allowing you the opportunity to recreate yourself anew.

CHAPTER 6

Importance of Rest, Centering, and Interlude

The Wonders of Rest Periods and Interludes and Their Exercises

Rest is essential after work, as it is necessary for optimal health. It is also biblically recorded that God created the earth in six days and rested on the seventh.

Getting your rest is just as vital as the exercises and activities discussed in this lecture, most notably that a resting period allows the regeneration and renewal of the necessary energy needed for balance and sustenance. Rest will improve our mental health, cardiovascular health systems, and many other systems of the body.

Most vacations taken worldwide by working-class people are for relaxation, mind refreshing, and recouping their strength and energy required to go back to work.

Researchers from the University of Pittsburgh Mind-Body Center found that leisure, including vacation, contributed to a more positive mindset and a dramatically lower level of clinical depression. Psychology Today, accessed November 29, 2019.

Researcher Karen Matthews from the same university, using data from the famous Framingham Heart Study, which followed about 12,000 men between ages 35 and 57 at risk of heart disease for nine years, found a correlation between how long the men lived and the length of their vacations. Those who took a more extended vacation appear to live longer.

Centering after a spiritual exercise and meditation is like taking a mini-vacation from the vigorous activities of the body, mind, and soul. It is a method of stabilizing or grounding the physical body to prevent a hangover effect on the body.

According to the constitution of a person, there are many other bodies apart from the physical, visible body. Most people commonly recognize two classifications, such as the physical and spiritual bodies. Still, in reality, there are five primary bodies: the physical body, the astral/emotional body, the mental body, the etheric body, and the soul body. During exercise, the normal fundamental vibration of the body can be raised into any of these corresponding bodies.

Those with specialized training can bring back memories, ideas, and feelings of their experiences while out in these bodies during meditation and spiritual exercises, which requires a form of centering to readjust the body to the typical day-to-day reality. Grounding helps you feel centered, calm, and peaceful.

From another perspective, centering transfers energy from the noisy left brain to the quiet right brain, which reduces anxiety and increases awareness of the present moment.

The Magic of Interlude During Meditation

In Biblical terms, God rested on the seventh day after creation... but before creation was an interlude.

Elijah, in the Christian Bible, only found God in the quiet whisper that came after the distracting occurrences of the mundane world, such as a fire and an earthquake. Our ordinary world is full of distracting elements that can make you lose sight of where you're going if you're not paying attention. Listening for the quiet interludes, seizing the opportunity to connect with the Divine, and using that connection productively, is spiritually refreshing.

Mystics, both Eastern and Western, especially Pythagoras, Milarepa, Jalaluddin Rumi, and many others, use the interlude for works of creativity and during healing practices, in the forms of physical or absent healing.

Interlude has a magic of its own, which helps in the execution of desired objectives, particularly when done for the benefit of others and the world.

Exercise on Interlude

- **Step 1**
  Sit comfortably in a chair with hands on your lap.

- **Step 2**
  Recite a brief prayer of protection or chant of your choice and visualize your Spiritual Guide. If a Christian, visualize Christ as much as you can and see it as real and complete.

- **Step 3**
  Take a slow deep breath through the nose. Do this slowly.

- **Step 4**
  Hold as long as you comfortably can, focusing on the spiritual, unselfish work you want to do.

- **Step 5**
  Breathe out slowly through the nose for as long as you can.

- **Step 6**
  Expel your breath for as long as you comfortably can, while visualizing the work as completed.

> *Note: This method has variations involving counting when breathing in, holding it, and exhaling. Some inhale for a count of 5 to 10, hold for 6 to 12 counts, and expel for 5 to 10 counts. (Count breath only if tolerated under the supervision of a knowledgeable teacher familiar with this method. Counting is not for everyone. The simple process given above is beneficial enough without counting breaths)*

- **Step 7**

Recite a brief closing prayer or chant of your choice, and see yourself centered and back in your body. Thank your Spiritual Guide or Christ, if a Christian, for allowing you to be a coworker in creation.

Dismiss, while seeing the desired result as completed without a doubt.

CHAPTER 7

The Power of Concentration and Use of Affirmations During Exercise

Effects of Concentration and Affirmation During Exercise

The importance of concentration and use of affirmation in furthering your goals and achievements is indisputable. Focus and attention are the keys to success in every endeavor. A scattered mind has difficulty achieving tasks.

> *"If you do not change direction, you may end up where you are heading."*
> — **Lao Tzu**

For anyone who is easily distracted and unable to concentrate, practicing exercises that help improve concentration is recommended for an optimal result when attempting to use any form of affirmation. For positive results, whether materially or spiritually, focused attention and concentration are essential.

Concentration and attention are vital to prayers and

meditation; likewise, the use of affirmation in achieving the desired result. Words are powerful instruments capable of being used creatively or destructively.

Words can condition the human aura and attract positive or negative attributes. They have the power to bless and the power to curse. Spoken words become more potent when used with intent.

The power embedded in the spoken word is one of the most magnificent instruments ever made by our Creator and used by masters of all ages. Our speech carries the energy of our intent with it. Speaking brings that which is concealed in our thoughts into outer manifestation.

Oftentimes, we are victims of our own thoughts and speech. We affirm ourselves to failure and sickness unconsciously by using the wrong language, whether in thought or spoken.

As a child, I witnessed the effects of destructive words used in an environment, and later, its adverse effects. There was a house on the opposite side of the road from where I grew up. It is not coincidental that people die in that house every two to three months. We often heard them wailing that someone had died. One of my friends who lived in this house also died at a tender young age of about 12.

Speech is one of the greatest weapons ever used for constructive or destructive purposes. We must continue to learn how to rebuild relationships and atone for karmic debts we we incur through negative speech.

Speech opens doors of communication in the physical, ethereal, and spiritual realms. It is critical we learn the proper way of communicating using the right speech, as we are karmically bound to every word we speak. What goes around surely comes around. Words of hate, anger, or destruction as well as words of love and creativity all have karmic implications—some too heavy to bear.

Rather, we should seize the opportunity to harness the power of positive speech in rebuilding our inner and outer lives through the use of affirmations. These work in conjunction with our subconscious to create desired positive outcomes.

During exercise, the triple effect of action, concentration, and affirmation has an extraordinary impact. This arouses the energy centers of our body and keeps them aligned with our mental faculties, while at the same time invoking the divine energy of the soul through visualization to trigger the desired results.

Exercise can be walking or on a treadmill using phrases such as:

- "I am wealthy and healthy."
- "My life is a miracle every day in every way,"
- "I am a divine soul,"
- "I am looking better and feeling better day by day in every way," and
- "Divine Light, light up my life and dispel all forms of shadows of negativity."

Use these affirmations w hile visualizing a positive outcome, called the "as-if attitude."

Replacement exercise is one method of improving focus and the ability to concentrate. You simply practice eliminating a preconceived notion or task by using mindfulness techniques. Forgo thinking up front of your like or dislike of a situation. The event or encounter becomes more manageable by using an affirmation to detach yourself from a preconceived outcome. This helps you direct your thoughts and energy on the goals of the scenario at hand. On its own, the affirmation is capable of replacing other distractors.

Replacement Exercise for Improving Focus and Attention

- **Step 1**
Intentionally minimize or eliminate physical distractions surrounding you.

- **Step 2**
Rid your mind of unnecessary, nagging thoughts and replace them with simple affirmations, as described above.

- **Step 3**
Ensure you have adequate time to rest.

- **Step 4**
Consistently adding simple meditation to your routine at the same time every day, even for 5 to 10 minutes, helps train your mind over time.

CHAPTER 8

The Healing Effects of Fasting When Combined with Exercise

While fasting, as commonly understood by many in spiritual terms, means giving up food or other worldly things for a period of time for spiritual reasons, it is worthwhile to know there are three main categories of fasting, such as physical food fasting, emotional fasting, and mental or spiritual fasting.

Many people may engage in one form of fasting or another, or practice them all simultaneously for many reasons such as detoxification, weight loss, to instill discipline, or for purification purposes. Regardless of the motives for the practice, fasting has been part of the holistic health and wellness practice of many who appear healthy, look younger than their ages, and appear vibrant and dynamic. After all, our bodies, minds, and spirits are connected and in close contact.

Although traditional dietary and detox advice is common today, forced diets and the use of detox materials do not achieve the same things a physical food fast, emotional fast, and mental fast do. Periodic food fasting, emotional fasting, and mental fasting help with the alignment processes by clearing and purifying the centers in the body and rendering them free of energy blockages that inhibit spiritual communication and impede the healing process.

Motion is an intrinsic part of any human activities, the driving force of life and existence. When combined with exercise, food, emotional, and/or mental fasting provide the fuel needed for opening the spiritual centers in a person. This produces proper alignment, focused attention, and engagement with the healing forces of nature. The healing properties of nature are further expedited when simple breathing exercises are combined with fasting and exercise.

Emotional and mental fasting include abstaining from any negative emotional activities, such as anger, fear, and gossiping, but rather blessing others and providing love. Mental fasting adds meditation and contemplating positive affirmations and spiritual literature within a certain period of time. Engaging in such practices helps alter the roots of karmic patterns that may be the source of certain conditions that are not diagnosable or reachable by current medical practices.

Mental fasting and mental or spiritual exercise are capable of building positive auras around its practitioners, dissolving past and present karma, while aligning themselves to the Divine Intelligence for simultaneous healing of the body. Herein lies the mystery of some of the healings that are beyond human understanding.

> *Note: Before engaging in any food fast, consult with your physician to get proper medical advice, especially if you have a medical condition that can be impacted by such a fast.*

CHAPTER 9

Powerful Holistic Exercises of Energy Centers Transformation

Complete healing and miracles are possible through the focus and blessings of the energy centers in the human body. This is one of the secrets of personal transformation and healing that has been practiced by many of the masters of ageless wisdom and kept hidden, but has miraculously found its way into the modern-day techniques used by a few who understand its effect. Please note that this technique is only suggested for healing purposes only— that is, for cleaning the centers of certain blockages, and not for the purpose of developing special powers or reaching a higher potential. Some misunderstand and think the highest potential can only be reached by going above the lower centers and using the higher centers of the body.

Rather, the energy centers are each considered little brains, as they all have a consciousness of their own and emit lights of different wavelengths and color. Sometimes through our attachments and habitual use of wrong emotions, we prevent the proper working of these centers and create blockages that lower the energy centers and degrade our lives.

Many report sudden healing and miracles when their centers are cleaned through certain actions they took, either through atonements for what they have done, fasting, prayer, or surrendering completely to the Divine Power that creates all. Most especially, when their consciousness changes during expressions of love and gratitude, forgiving themselves and others, eliminating fear, and just simply surrendering. Healing, as expressed by many, came without any logical explanation. Many call it grace, forgiveness of their sins, or the dissolving of karma.

Irrespective of what this is attributed to, scientists recognized something intriguing and special when such people were examined clinically. It was discovered through significant research and testing that the energy centers of those involved in these types of miracles show a type of balance and coherence otherwise not seen in diseased humans or affected organs of the body. After each healing experience, there appeared to be a radiant light emanating from the healed person and their affected organs.

Each of the human energy centers are under the control of the autonomic nervous system of the body. Mystics and masters of wisdom over the years have been using several meditation techniques to change the frequency and energy patterns of their body and energy centers, ridding themselves of unwanted energy that creates abnormal patterns capable of causing diseases and ailments of the body. Such negative energy patterns create incoherence in the centers, which58can be reversed into coherence.

Scientists are now capable of measuring such coherence and incoherence in the laboratory and have examined this in volunteers examined before and after the exercises.

Presented below is an exercise that has been used by many healers and masters for clearing center blockages, increasing their energy vibrations and frequencies through concentrating on each energy center and the fields around them, while simultaneously bringing in harmonious energy of forgiveness, love, and gratitude during the blessing of those centers.

- **Step 1**
  Find a comfortable place to sit with your back supported.

- **Step 2**
  If you are a Christian or of a particular faith, you may say a prayer of your choice if you choose.

- **Step 3**
  Focus on the sex organ area, the inferior mesenteric plexus. Focus in the area, feel the surrounding energy around the area. Be nonjudgmental and do not concentrate on past experiences involving the area. Simply acknowledge the presence, bless the area, show gratitude that you are a life and able to bless the area. Elevate your thoughts to gratitude and joy and love without resentments and this will help create coherence in the area and remove blockages.

- **Step 4**
  Repeat this for the next center, the digestive glands and the pancreatic glands as we did above, blessing they are and then show gratitude and blessing the area while expressing love and joy to help raise the vibration of the area.

- **Step 5**

Repeat this step with the other centers from adrenal to thymus, thyroid, pineal, pituitary gland, and the imaginary center above the head called the thousand-petal lotus or Ka.

- **Step 6**

Visualize the space around your whole body as being surrounded by a powerful energy field as with a magnet. See it and feel it.

- **Step 7**

Take a slow, deep breath, let it out slowly and dismiss the exercise from your mind. Relax for approximately 5 to 10 minutes after the exercise.

CHAPTER 10

Healing Yourself and Manifesting Through Quantum Technique

The year of 1926 heralded the laws of quantum physics as differentiated from the previous Newtonian physics. Quantum physics is simply stated as the study of matter and energy at the most fundamental level. It uncovers the properties and behaviors of the building blocks of nature, of matter and the behavior of matter, and the energy in and around matter.

The principles espoused by quantum physics have been known, practiced, and utilized for years by mystics and spiritual masters of the ageless wisdom. Many have defied the laws of physics as it was known to us then, through occurrences recorded surrounding their lives. Masters such as Milarepa, Apollonius of Tyana, Pythagoras, and the masters who built such structures as the pyramids of Egypt and many other legacies that have scientists globally still scratching their heads, trying to figure out how many of the structures left behind for humanity were built and how their miraculous feats were performed.

One of the major principles of quantum physics that revolves around transforming and changing who we are and manifesting what we need for survival on this planet is that all possibilities in the quantum field exist in the present moment as electromagnetic potential. There are infinite possibilities in every moment. Living in the *now*, rather than living in the past or in the future, allows us to tap into the abundant possibilities that exist at any moment.

Many carry the baggage of their past into the present, or daydream about the future and the fear of getting there, that they are paralyzed and unable to put the present—this very moment— into action before it fades away. The energy of shifting your mind from past to present to future dissipates the energy of the present moment and prevents tapping into its full potential because where you place your attention is also where you place your energy.

Combining our discussions on energy from the previous chapters on maintaining an 'as-if attitude,' see yourself as already in the situation you desire and bring yourself with all your senses to live in the present and be aware of it, moment to moment. Combining this with the principles of fact presented by the quantum principle, bringing a clear intention of whatever we plan to do or attain into the moment and balancing it with the intensity of our emotions creates a positive energy pattern that aids in its accomplishment, rather than when the emotion is absent.

This goes along with the principles of the Holy Bible that say when you praying to God for anything, you should see yourself as already having received it, as the mind and the emotions of feeling of receiving, apart from showing a superior faith and trust in the Divine that is called for, also helps create an invisible energy field that aids in the manifestation.

Exercise: Using the quantum method, put the moment to use when you need something or are praying for a manifestation.

- Remove preconceived ideas of the past and thoughts of difficulties of the future from your mind.
- Remove thoughts of difficulties getting the things or the barriers between you and what you need as much as possible as nothing is impossible for the divine in you. This moment is for your manifestation and your accomplishment. You are using this moment of blessing to enrich yourself and those you care about.

Put the moment you allotted for the exercise to use as follows:

- Say a brief prayer of your choice if you are a Christian
- Combine *concentrated, clear intention* with *feelings of receipt and gratitude* to create a **special quantum blessing** and opportunity that will propel you toward your request and goal. This special quantum divine energy, once set in motion, continues to work on your behalf, whether you are awake or sleeping, aware of it or not.
- Dismiss the entire process from your mind after the exercise, trusting that it is done and continue with your goals in a normal fashion

without thinking about the exercise for the day or worrying about its effects.

You can repeat the procedure daily, especially in the morning or at night when conditions are calm and your energy centers are active

CHAPTER 11

Conclusion

There is a famous saying: "What you don't use, you lose." Just as this is true regarding everything on the physical planes of existence, this assertion is likewise true for everything relating to our other body systems, whether physical, emotional, mental, or spiritual.

Our bodies are vitalized by energies that are in constant motion within and without. We live in a world of moving energies, whether you realize it or not. Motion and activity are the essence of life. Rigidity brings pain and suffering. We have to keep moving.

Life is never static. It keeps changing over time. As your environment changes, look for ways to adapt and catch up with it; otherwise, you'll be left behind. A changing environment can take your job and your life with it unless you adapt to keep your body, mind, and soul intact.

In 1982, AutoCAD was introduced. This computer application enabled architects to design electronically rather than drawing plans by hand. Those who refused to learn AutoCAD soon found themselves out of a job.

This same principle explains why Circuit City, Radio Shack, Sears, Toys 'R Us, and many other brick-and-mortar stores went out of business and thousands of workers lost their jobs when online sales exploded: they failed to adapt.

That which brings pain and suffering in the physical plane of existence soon depresses the mind, causing fear and anxiety that, in turn, distracts attention from the soul. There are opportunities embedded in pain and suffering, which few might not recognize during their period of agony but see clearly in hindsight.

Activities and movements that correlate to being adaptable on the physical plane include studying your surroundings and trends. Part of life is to keep learning and evolving as new things emerge. We only stop learning when we die.

As long as we are alive in the physical body, we have to keep our brain cells active by learning new things and new ways of doing things and adapting quickly as the laws of motion determine whether we live or die. Our ability to change defines our survival in any realm of existence.

Just as it is in the physical plane, so it is in the emotional, mental, and spiritual planes. We cannot be lukewarm in spirit. Our capacity to love and to help others should increase each day. Our ability to engage in spiritual soul movement and travel to other spiritual realms of existence needs to grow, most notably as the physical body is wearing out, and our earthly mission is near its end.

Everyone will die someday, whether rich or poor, regardless of gender, color, or country of origin. But death doesn't need to be feared because, as Saint Francis expressed it, "It is in dying that we are born to eternal life." This means that without death there is no birth. Then we continue to learn to "die daily" as Saint Peter expressed it in the Holy Bible. It is just like putting a seed in the ground to grow. Before the germination process can take place, the outer shell must diminish to make way for the new life.

It is no surprise that many people today do not remember the telephone number of their immediate friends and family because of their dependency on cell phones. The ability to do such a simple memory recall as a phone number is gone because the memory cells in this area of the brain are no longer being used and no longer active, as atrophy has set in.

In no time, a disease of the mind and spirit will have an outward manifestation. The objective, in most cases, is determined by the subjective. True, complete healing comes from within outward and not vice versa. When we are dead within, we'll soon find the physical body dead as well. The aura seen days, weeks, and even months before means the person also knows as they transition.

I have had the opportunity to be around many dying people of all faiths and spiritual backgrounds as I worked in many hospitals, nursing facilities, and rest homes, initially as a caregiver and later as a consultant. I have worked with clients who were very peaceful and always smiling when dying. Some even died with smiles on their faces as they made the transition into the other world, escaping the mortal shell of the body left behind.

I have also had the chance to work with some who predicted the exact day and even time of their death. "Don't worry," a lady told one of the hospice workers, "You guys work so hard, but God told me a few minutes ago that He is taking me away from earth at 3 a.m. tomorrow," she said, smiling while reciting the rosary.

The hospice aide working with her was nervous and came running to tell the staff. I happened to be the supervisor on duty that day. Everyone thought the client was delusional.

The night supervisor who was supposed to relieve me from duty at 11 p.m. called in sick that night. I stayed and worked a double shift to supervise the night staff. At 11 p.m., the formal hospice caregiver went home, and a new one came on duty to work with this client overnight. As I was busy completing some paperwork, the overnight hospice worker asked me to come examine this client she was caring for, as "something is going on with her," she reiterated with a fearful look on her face. My first reaction was to look at the time clock hanging above my head. It was precisely 3 a.m. I ran to the client's room to find her passing away with a smile on her face. I examined her and did the final preparatory procedure to make the pronouncement.

I witnessed many clients who were afraid of dying. They were frightened while leaving their physical bodies even until the last hour and minute of their death. Some keep calling out and want everyone in their room at that time. Others become very agitated and require medication to help with the relaxation process. I have always wondered why there are such differences in these situations. One person is smiling, and fully relaxed, while another is frightened. Is this due to acceptance of death, or other conditions unknown, a rational mind wonders.

Sometimes those with smiles on their faces were previously in pain. Then, at a later time, it appeared that some buffer prevented the experience of pain, and only smiles manifested as the soul faded away from the mortal body.

As Elizabeth Kubler-Ross said in her book on death and dying, we all have something to learn from the dying patient. There are lots of things the dying have to teach doctors, nurses, clergy, their families—all of us.

The focus of this book is not for comparison or that of declaring a particular method of escaping the physical body as invalid. It is also not that of preference for a particular faith or spiritual affiliation. Alternatively, through my observation over the years, I have discovered that those who engage in some form of physical, mental, and spiritual exercises appeared to depart from the physical shell of the body more easily and peacefully than others.

Meditation and spiritual exercises, after all, are a form of temporary death to the physical world. Saint Peter in the Bible said he dies daily to life in the body.

My biological father was said to be singing and mentioning all his children's names while escaping the carnal body. He was singing that God may let us meet again while he was in transition. His early life was that of constant physical activities, spiritual exercises, and service to God. He served in the church and the town, helping many families and children in every form.

He recited his rosary every night and every morning while alive. He rang his bell for morning prayers every day at 5 am and evening prayers every night at 9 pm. "The family that prays together stays together," he always said as he rang the bell for everyone to join in prayer. He invited the neighbors who showed an interest and wanted to participate voluntarily.

While I was at home with him, I heard him day and night doing mental meditation using the prayer of Saint Patrick:

> Christ with me,
> Christ before me,
> Christ behind me,

Christ in me,
Christ on my right,
Christ on my left,
Christ when I lie down,
Christ when I sit down,
Christ when I arise,
Christ in the heart of every man who thinks of me,
Christ in every eye that sees me,
Christ in every ear that hears me.

I could hear him day and night reciting this prayer. Many times, he recited this prayer when he was taking a shower, sometimes at 2 a.m. when he was getting some work done. I later found out it was St. Patrick's Breastplate. He died around the age of 110.

Witnessing this at an early age, I had the opportunity to recognize the same pattern in other dying clients while reviewing the history of their earthly life.

I observed that this is also present in others of different spiritual faiths, nationalities, and affiliations. I found it in those who devoted themselves to certain forms of activities, and who practiced some virtues that kept them active physically and spiritually, energizing and purifying not only their physical bodies, but also their minds and spirits.

> **The path of the godly leads to life. So why fear death?**
> **– Proverbs 12:28**

Those who knew these people attested to how their life was lived. Not only what they did physically, but also the effects of their thoughts, their words, and minds were carefully controlled and guarded spiritually. Many actively engaged in meditation and other spiritual activities such as prayer and contemplation to uplift their souls to the highest spiritual realms. They were eager to help others above themselves while on this earthly stage.

This work has covered many different exercise techniques, ranging from those dealing with the physical and immortal bodies to the emotions, mind, soul, and spirit. Essentially, they provide alternatives to your old habits. If you find yourself attracted to one area more than another, it may show an imbalance in an area of your body.

Engaging in exercises beyond the physical body helps invigorate us and keeps our bodies in proper alignment. Incorporating exercises involving the body, mind, and spirit into our daily practices helps to balance our body energy systems, allowing us to enjoy complete and absolute healing of our bodies. It alerts the body's cells, organs, and energy centers to our awareness that the sustenance of the physical body comes from a higher spiritual source within, far greater than any human imagination.

When we as people are able to engage in a state of higher consciousness far above even meditation, forgetting the instrument used, and just be, then we are granted even more opportunities to experience and explore those states of higher consciousness beyond where meditation alone can reach.

> **"These, then, are my last words to you:**
> **Be not afraid of life.**
> **Believe that life is worth living**
> **and your belief will help you create that fact."**
> **– William James, 1800's psychologist**

FURTHER READING

American College of Sports Medicine. (2003). *ACSM Fitness Book*, 3rd ed. Champaign, IL: Human Kinetics.

Anderson, B., & Anderson, J. (2000). *Stretching, 20th Anniversary Revised Edition*. Bolinas, CA: Shelter Publications.

Bodger, C. (1998). *Smart Guide to Getting Strong & Fit*. Hoboken, NJ: John Wiley & Sons.

Bonifonte, S.P. (2004). *Tai Chi for Seniors: How to Gain Flexibility, Strength, and Inner Peace*. Franklin Lakes, NJ: New Page Books. Desjardins, S., & Tanguay-Labonté, M. (2018). The Effects of Physical Activity on Sleep among Adolescents and Adults: A Narrative Review. *Journal of Sleep and Sleep Disorder Research-* 1(2):42-59.

Dworkis, S., & Moline, P. (1994). *ExTension: The 20-Minute-a-Day, Yoga-Based Program to Relax, Release & Rejuvenate the Average Stressed-Out Over-35-Year-Old Body*. New York: Poseidon Press.

Finger, A., & Bingham, A. (2000). *Introduction to Yoga: A Beginner's Guide to Health, Fitness, and Relaxation*. New York: Three Rivers Press.

Gerrish, M. (1999). *When Working Out Isn't Working Out: A Mind/Body Guide to Conquering Unidentified Fitness Obstacles*. New York: St. Martin's Griffin.

Jain, S., Hammerschlag, R., Mills, P., Cohen, L., Krieger, R.,

Vieten, C., & Lutgendorf, S.K. (2015). Clinical Studies of Biofield Therapies: Summary, Methodological Challenges, and Recommendations. *Global Advances in Health and Medicine, 4*, 58-66 (Suppl).

Katz, J. & Bruning, N.P. (1993). *Swimming for Total Fitness: A Progressive Aerobic Program.* New York: Main Street Books.

Kennedy, M.M., & Newton, M. (1997). Effect of exercise intensity on mood in step aerobics. *Journal of Sports Medicine & Physical Fitness.* 37(3):200–204.

Klemp, H. (1993). *The Spiritual Exercises of ECK.* Minneapolis: Eckankar.

Lindahl, J. R., Fisher, N.E., Cooper, D.J., Rosen, R.K., & Britton, W.B. (2017). The varieties of contemplative experience: A mixed-methods study of meditation-related challenges in Western Buddhists. *PloS one.* 12(5):e0176239 http://www.doi.org/10.1371/journal.pone.0176239

Meyers, C. (1992). *Walking: A Complete Guide to the Complete Exercise.* New York: Random House.

Ohayon, M., Wickwire, E.M., Hirshkowitz, M., et al. (2017) National Sleep Foundation's sleep quality recommendations: first report. *Sleep Health.* 3(1): 6-19.

Reddy, J., & Roy S. (2019). Understanding Meditation Based on the Subjective Experience and Traditional Goal: Implications for Current Meditation Research. *Frontiers in Psychology,* 10.

Rones, R., & Silver, D. (2007). *Sunrise Tai Chi: Simplified Tai Chi for Health & Longevity.* Boston: YMAA Publication Center, Inc. *Science Daily.* March 20, 1998. Tai Chi Lowers Blood Pressure for Older Adults.

Roney-Dougal, S.M., Ryan, A., & Luke, D. (2013). The relationship between local geomagnetic activity, meditation, and psi. Part 1: Literature review and theoretical model. *Journal of the Society for Psychical Research*. 77(2):72-88.

Shephard, R.J. (1997). Exercise and relaxation in health promotion. *Sports Medicine*. Auckland, NZ, 23(4):211-217.

Sobel, D., & Ornstein, R. (1996). *The Healthy Mind, Healthy Body Handbook*. New York: Time Life Medical.

Stutz J., Eiholzer R., & Spengler C.M. (2019). Effects of Evening Exercise on Sleep in Heathy Participants: A Systematic Review and Meta-Analysis. *Sports Medicine*. Auckland, N.Z. 49(2):269-287. https://doi.org/10.1007/s40279-018-1015-0

Wang, F., & Boros, S. (2019). The effect of physical activity on sleep quality: a systematic review. *European Journal of Physiotherapy*. 23:1, 11-18https://doi.org/10.1080/21679169.2019.1623314

www.ingramcontent.com/pod-product-compliance
Lightning Source LLC
Chambersburg PA
CBHW051236120626
46547CB00013B/1672